R A JORDAN
In Three Parts

Published in the United States by House of Walker Publishing, LLC (HWP) Elizabeth, New Jersey 07208

All rights Reserved. No part of this publication may be reproduced or transmitted in any form or by any means, electronic or mechanical, including photocopying, recording, or any other information storage or retrieval system, without the written permission from the publisher, House of Walker Publishing, LLC

Permissions: Manuscript presented by: James E. Jordan
Cover art by: Jordan Chambers
Library of Congress Control Number: 2018952716
Copyright © 2018 by James E. Jordan
ISBN: 978-0-9834762-9-0
LCCN: 2021900109

In memory of my mother, Ethel Marie Jordan, who saw the better in us, and pointed us to the more.

With Gratitude

I want to express my sincere gratitude to all who helped and encouraged me to move on compiling my late brother's poetic works. Time and space do not allow for all to be mentioned. Monica Verona and Joel Tucciarone, among those closest to my brother, provided continual encouragement. The late Susan Doherty, who initiated the compilation, provided the groundwork I needed to follow through. And lastly, Michelle Nelson, at House of Walker Publishing, provided the apparatus to complete it.

TABLE OF CONTENTS

Introduction

Part I – Dedications

Anecdote For Holland Sherba	1
Dust of Dreams – Proverbs 14:12 For David Wesner	3
For Winnie Verona at Seventy-Five	6
A Dark Chorus of Angels – Psalm 8:4 For Joel Tucciarone	8
Revelation of Onyx For Artie Thompson	13
These Shall Return Without Her For Luz Nieves	15
To the Musicians	17
To My Father – Through Strength	18
To the Reader (Little Offerings)	21

Part II – Observations

A Man in Minor Mode	25
A Mountain Bears This Grief	27
An Idea of More Than We Can See	28
But Night Is Not Enough To Satisfy	29
Death by Air	31
Death Prelude	33
For the Year's End	34
In Consideration Of	35
Lady Nova	36
Light Exuberance	37
Love's Lyric	38

Mrs. Noe Meets Richard Wagner	39
The Moment of Each Step	40
The Necessity That Requires	42
Nor Light Reflecting Orb	43
Now the Fattest Poverty	44
October Greets the Virgins	45
Regressive Biography	46
Stop Midwinter to Consider	47
That We Should Fast for A	48
Thank God for the Passage of Time	50
That Would Be and Would Be Born	51
These Will Return Without Her	52
Through Love Illumined	54
Through This First Maturity	56
Woman's Words Are All of One	57
Words of Herself	63
Untitled (Titled by James E. Jordan):	
A Black Bird's Domain	64
Bagatelle	70
Bliss	71
Ebony Queen	72
Fuel for Time	73
Give What We Cannot	74
Her Reply of No	75
It May Be October	76
The Man in His Room	77
Perhaps	79

Sacrifice	80

Part III – Revelations

A Last Word for Lazarus – St. John XI	83
A Man Was Caught Up and Saw – II Corinthians 12:1-4	86
Before the Final Gold	91
The Days Are Passing Strange	93
Divine Characters	94
Elegy	96
Of An Elegy (A Moment After)	97
Genesis 11:4	99
Light Crescendo	100
Made Greater	101
November Light	102
Think of This, Then That	103
Thirty Three Preludes – For My Father	104
Thus Shall the Angels Be Judged	115
Toward Heavenly Credence	116
A Word to Mrs. Noe	124
Untitled (Titled by James E. Jordan):	
Both Judge and Advocate	125
Eve	126
Eve II	127
The Lovers Lost	128
James Edward Jordan	129

Introduction

On November 7, 1954, the water broke and the birth pangs came. The child was born; and as life went on, so did the pressure to conform. However, this one did not conform, nor did he ever stay 'in the box'.

This nonconformist was my brother, Rodenick Anthony Jordan (aka R A Jordan or Jordan). Born in Mobile, Alabama to Ethel Marie Sims and Lee Andrew Jordan Jr. and raised on Milwaukee Wisconsin's tough, northwest side.

My late father recalled when he and my brother were in downtown Milwaukee, around 1960. My brother engaged a nearby stranger. Him being all of five or six at the time, began to expound on some complex theory/observation. Upon the conclusion of his discourse, the man was so moved that he reached into his pocket and give my brother a shiny dime!

In high school, Jordan chose learning German after rejecting the narrow-minded recommendation of the Milwaukee Public School system's faculty, "Blacks have an easier time with Spanish." Physical limitations would cause the left-handed man choose the violin over brass and woodwinds; and as a result, he rejected rhythm and blues for classical music. This earned him scorn and ridicule within the 1960s, 1970s black community.

After studying orchestration at the University of Wisconsin-Milwaukee, Jordan relocated to New York City, where he studied at Manhattan School of Music. This led to earning a chair in an orchestra company located in Caracas, Venezuela. After the orchestra company became defunct, he relocated to San Francisco and later returned to Milwaukee.

Maintaining his wry sense of humor, my brother shared an encounter he had on Milwaukee's East Side. This time it was the early 1980s. He was dining with a friend in a restaurant and gained the attention of a man sitting nearby. The man took issue with my brother being the only black person in the establishment.

The man stood to his feet and came up to my brother. The man leaned into his face with a smirk and said, "Hey, did you know that some black people are almost as good as white people?" My brother, responding as only he could, "And some are even better!" After a moment, my brother's close friend persuaded him they needed to get up and get out. An unfortunate encounter on what still remains Milwaukee's most cosmopolitan side.

In 1985, Jordan returned to New York City; and developed a love and passion for poetry.

One day, around the late 1980s, a small group of German sailors wandered aimlessly along New York City's Park Avenue. At just the right time, this enigmatic man took note of their predicament and approached them. After a brief inquiry, he provided the sailors with clear instructions to their destination—in German no less! Leaving the sailors more elated than they were previously lost.

Time and space do not allow to tell all. His untimely death took place on March 26, 1998, in Harlem, New York.

The above is a brief glimpse into who R. A. Jordan was; and so the following compilation of this poetry.

Part I
Dedications

Anecdote

(For Holland Sherba)

One late evening a good friend said
Having children is the greatest thing
He's done so far in life
No broad success or continuing fame
He enjoys both
Are equal to the fun of fatherhood and marriage
Certainly his sons came by love's easy course
Yet he thinks he ought to thank God
Or whatever power gives us gifts of life
He told me how his first-born boy
Not yet three
Seems to take simple things to know the world
Just about every night as strength and curiosity
Have lengthened his grasp
He carries a rock or pebble jagged plain
Shiny or smooth to bed with him
Something of the common earth
Which must seem so overwhelming
He almost always ends an afternoon's play
With a search for such and
He's got a small box nearly full of rocks
Once he asked a question that was answered no
Rocks have never been alive
And no they haven't died

Only living things are able to die
Other childish questions followed
How are dying and death explained to one so young
When someone dies most of what they really are
The best part of what they are
Is taken away and cannot come back
And the part that's left behind
Is forever changed in a sad angry way
And can never do again the things living people do
Death is a kind of long sad sleep
But little boys shouldn't think too much about it
But my friend went on that his boy thought a lot about it
When one day at dinner he caught the fresh eyes
Of a couple of whole boiled trout
At once delicious and slightly grotesque
Lying on the platter
In their silvery scented skin
And each time a tender filet was lifted away
Those hard eyes glittered with the rooms abundant light
Somehow charming the child in a familiar way
Because later that night my friend discovered
That instead of the usual backyard gem
He held a fish eye in his little clenched fist.

Dust of Dreams

Proverbs 14:12

For David Wesner

I

Observe from this vantage
The muted tragedy of distant stars
That flare to reach beyond themselves
Toward the imagined primacy
That immediate heaven
Might be theirs to hold alone
To loom upon the horizon
To burn away blue spectrums of atmosphere
To be more luminous white
Brightening moons of remotest skies
Seem the depraved starry ambition
What worlds of estimable intelligence
That have made a romance of moonlight
Or perceive the nova's fatal gesture
Speculate upon such or surmise
That such comprise a tragedy
It is more to wonder for whom is it tragic
Or that a man took the all
Of this celestial passion play
For inspiration.

II

It breathed

The whole light of night around him

Then refreshed and mastered its world

With a new designation of objects

Capped and completed by naming things thus

This was to create as

It was a man who would not compound

The wheezing fugue of his fellows and

Upon his enterprise, he measured and gleaned

Wisdom from the point of truth

However, he became more the professor and scholar

Of what was believed with the bliss of it.

All of a paradise he desired

In its time the light he breathed became intrinsic

And a gift given to favored kin

It made a myth of his prime coruscation

Of men suffered with different light

Its point of reference severely despised

It became wholly self-reverential

He was the celebration of himself

And ubiquitous

Of time there was no fear

Time was the sense of hope

And maturation

The moment but a trilling appoggiatura toward
The eternal magnitude of his race.

III

Genius and the mind of heaven
Are the same and one
More than an intelligence
Proffered by the sun
The light of genius faded finally
All the might of him
Wizened men thinking
Think his earthy flame
A photogene flashing before
Their minds' sleeping eye
Its voice held the air booming furiously once
"You would have me deified
But deity is superfluous
As we are sublime each in divine"
A sound that seemed more than the wind now
Blowing the blaze of his banners to tatters
There were men in columns
Who bore his colors and standards
But they are now fallen into the dust
Of its mannish dream.

For Winnie Verona At Seventy-Five

Upon the foyer

Of another year

The joy of life

Of a single life

Come flooding to mind

It may seem strange

That we should live

To fine maturity

And find that we have been favored

With rewards of grace

It may be with wonder

That we live longer still

To take pride

In our children now

As we did when they were babies

And again enjoy

That special gift

Of our children's children

The pleasures of a lifetime's love

In giving

Return to warm

Our wintry days

And comfort the mind

As it turns with thoughts

Of God's time

Beyond our own.

A DARK CHORUS OF ANGELS

(Psalm 8:4)

For Joel Tucciarone

But never
And never again
Toward the throne of stars
For now is my kingdom
Into your heart and mind
Established upon the power of the air
And forever afterward
More splendid mythology
Shall instruct history
To blur the details
Of our ancient monster
Whose excellent hand
Through mine
Is upon the world
And the Word spoken among man
And angels
Is broken and lost
Which is the Word of the kingdom
Your kingdom
That shall not come
And forever afterward

Man shall take impotent passion for love
For love is also lost
I have known the tongues of angels
And of man
As I am my god I am what man
Is not
And the end of what
He can never be
As I am my god I am the beginning
Of that which is won
Through one chaste
Unholy kiss
What world what gold
What infinite light of life and
Weight of glory
And grief
    Behold
    They are broken
As these wings of broken angels
Who could not know
What form of man
Would return or echo
The dreaming love song of Your
Mind and heart
At their breaking
Their knowledge was broken

And the deceleration began

Into time and desperation

With each life becoming smaller

Living through

The memory of what was

When memory

Is not resisted

    Before the daystar

Was set above us

We were the sons of morning and these wings

Crowded heaven when all was heaven

The sound of rejoicing was music for our dance

With the creatures that are jeweled with many eyes

And were in counterpoint against the ostinato chant

Of supreme holiness and grace

And the dance was light upon water

Brightening the music to silence

As the wings of the cherubim parted

To reveal that face of terror and beauty

Before which we fell

In joy of being one with the complex

Of efflorescent creation

    Now dark chorus of angels

Sing your hymn into our deep night

Few things we have known are true and console
As music is true.

    They who are broken
Shall put off brokenness
As they are now and forever
Becoming dim and invisible
Clothed in the very garment of heaven
Set far above us
The sons of mourning
These children
Each an iridescent jewel
Of the grace and favor denied us
Who are now and forever forsaken
Persecuted cast down destroyed
Under their judgment
They shall judge the angels
That weighs heavily upon us
Perplexed to despair
By these meek and furious exponents
Of the light
And they are the dance
Of light upon light
For there among them dancing is the act
Of the spirit in love
And they are the music

That returns and resounds

Constricting our dream

Of hope against hope

And yet we may still hope

After we are crowded

With our heirs

Beneath the blaze

And roaring waves

Of the eternal sea

    Amen

R. Jordan

Revelation of Onyx

(For Artie Thompson)

Allow these details

The place of myth

The god Onyx is fallen

At the word of unquestioned authority

And with his fall

Heaven's dark fabric is rent

Revealing the eternity

Behind the sky

Now there is such

Astonishing light

As if earth were

The center of a diamond

All mankind

Is mad with revelation

And staggers as this glory

Is pronounced

This is the world taken

Within heaven's full embrace

No longer in want

Of love's ambition

Nor turning slowly becoming cold

Men are angels with one mind

All their details

The place of myth.

These Shall Return Without Her

For Luz Nieves

With its façade
Of weathered grandeur,
The house maintains such dignity
Of a kind
Its mistress would approve,
Though she is now past caring.
Her thoughts are full of the natural order,
Not this small world of human design.
Her room's wide windows
Look to the south and
Open to a vista
Of garden and sky,
And of the trees
That were always her season.
It was beauty for her
To think them most beautiful now,
In their late autumn leaflessness.
Memories of the spring's
Copulative vigor,
Of summer's lush drapery.
Of the boughs green with gold,
Seemed less the things of her memory
And more like some fiction

She imagined had once been real.
The gray clouds
And graying land,
Seen beyond her bedroom windows,
Are a monochrome
Of her sleep and waking,
To such music the wind makes amid
The branches, brown and black.
But these were her peace
Not the red bird's return
To sing its florid hymns.
Rather the elegance,
The simple stark elegance,
Of intelligent trees, standing against
Winter's decree.

To the Musicians

Within the silence after music,
We believe that we have heard
Gold spun out of air.

We say gold to impart the value
Common to the mind of all.
And we liken it to air,

For nothing is so familiar or
Has such light and movement
And is yet so often sweet.

(For Dean H., Sharon H., Suzanne K., Cindy L., Linda G., Tommy N., and Mrs. Director, Barbara W.)

To My Father

THROUGH STRENGTH

And there

Drying between

The acts and dream of death in life

Are bones of an exiled people

And these would know a simple great thing:

Deeds that cling

From past to future tell

That a simple great thing is greater in itself

Than whatever great thing it has done

And this

Love began and brightens the dark glass

Reflecting the progress made against violent history

Through strength toward virtue

          Think of bones

Moving a man

With footsteps ordered toward the heart of God

Gifted of greater hands

Hurled stone to stone

And before his face fell beasts and thousands

But the man of such bones

Would not touch the life in evil anointed against him

To prevent his sudden glory

Think Again of Bones

Which once walked as a king
Briefly arrayed in breathless splendor
Divided in mind willful and wise
Governed and governing
Through words of enduring wonder
But the man of these bones
Chose beneath the fame of wisdom
To embrace the gilded vanities
Had in the kiss
Of dying lips
Think of bones

Neglected in whatever places
Gleaming with a look that questions:
Will we live yet again?
But the answer gnaws
And is the memory of lost opportunities offered
While their marrow was fresh
And encouraged the flesh
In whatever places they lay
Wrathful exhausted
Alone together
Perhaps fulfilled by an immediate wind
Lifted to sting the eyes of the generation maturing
Out of worlds common then strange

Born once to flesh and blood

To the new legacy contained in blood

Had in God's own promised advantage

Which spans the brief day and time

And proves experience no teacher of knowledge

Only had in part

To The Reader
(Little Offerings)

Here are my children.
So stricken with poverty

That they first recoil
At your gentle offer.

Of comfort, so strange
And strangely transforming

They have been mine,
But I give them to you.

Part II
Observations

A Man In Minor Mode

It made little difference, if people paid
Him compliments. It meant little to him
If people thought him a natty dresser, or

That he could be trusted with deepest confidence,
He felt he knew himself in a better way
Than any man ever has. Thus it was with glibness

Of ease, that he walked away his fellows.
But what of the soul's darkening, that he knew
Trepidations? His sense of self and of wellbeing,

The laugh with wide and whitened smile
Were things gleaned from the chameleon's art.
He worked its charm upon all he encountered, and

The knowledge of it was made certain and sure, in that
The sun and moon shone with like indifference –
No one had cause to look twice beneath the surface

Of what seemed to be. But the reasonable calm,
The apt virtuosity and presumptive air,
Were to crack his mirrored image.

The laugh, the smile, the furrowed brow
The whole stack of mock emotion,
The face that merely mimics them,

Because the necessity of frequent change,
As his manner became cause of wonder.
He understood, within a moment, what further

Knowledge required: such lessons learned
Of toads and chameleons, needs be compounded with light
Is the chameleon ever slow to adapt to its envisions?

Does it dimly perceive its climate, with camouflage?
An automatic action? Such light that men regard as
Intrinsic to man, burned faint and blue within him.

The divisible man of this distress
With the heart's howl behind, an affable calm
It must not be. Say rather, that darkness.

Be lengthened and drawn to shadow
By light, towards the ideal and fatal
Option and thus be subsumed.

A Mountain Bears This Grief

Maintain
What is the splendor
Of your bearing
Of your frosted crown
And silver peaks that define
The heaven's wealth of blue
How have you witnessed time?
And are yet ineffably timeless
Will your snows
Be shaken to earth?
Will your breath of coldest atmospheres
Descent to this valley
First to chill
Then to freeze
This lake to glacial calm
Its waters cannot reflect
Your height or wonder
They are deeply troubled and deepest red
The waves are crimson with the babies
Who would be and would be born.

An Idea of More Than We Can See

These peaks are only an idea of themselves.
The eternal idea and pretense of earth.
Its gleaming crown majestic. The lake
Before them, which pools at their base,
Is a surface that belies calm.

To reflect such height is to suggest great
Depth. The iced and silver crags, in their turn
Are the white that defines water's blue
Translucence. But the mountains are long
Apparent before the lake is seen.

Sapphire skies more appropriately
Frame the grandeur of this idea. But
The lake has enough within itself
To mirror the place and be content
To rest in the zest of its blue.

But Night Is Not Enough To Satisfy

He was in need of night,
Of the way heaven's darkened expanse

He thought to take a bit
Of the moon as a beacon

To light his journey's way,
The moonbeam seemed

A light more certain than that
Of his soul or mind's single eye.

As he was into the darkness,
The starry night's softest glistening.

Caressed and welcomed him,
Yet, still and more, he began

To covet the brightness of the nearest
Star. It (was) an intelligence (seemed)

That understood the need he had
To make a hermitage of the night.

He was far and high upon
Such hope as a start might proffer…

A mountain below, did chide
Its fellows and peevishly asked

How is a man able to fly so
Easily or even at all,

Above the bounds and mark
Our peaks have set for him…

Death by Air

Not by water, but by land. It is the princess
That shall come. The determined daughter
Of Poseidon's heirs, peer of porpoises

And tutelary of fish. She shall come against
Her father's will, although he knows well the need.
When the sirens' songs have ceased to entice,

Perhaps her sacrifice will succeed
Where threats and violent action have failed.
The lust and war of merchant-kings are in part

The cause of her distress. She shall come
After the cetacean's grief has become her own.
She will never be mother, nor shall she be

Given in marriage: her intended died at the hand
Of those that dwell upon the land. The watery world
Is all her love and all of love that she shall know.

But without the offering she must make, her domain
Shall be but watery waste. She shall come upon the morning
Tide, with her aquatic host. They will in sorrow watch

her wash up to shore, to drown and perish in the air…

This is the death by land and air. The sacrifice

That might preserve the life of the precious seas.

Death Prelude

The flowers know nothing

Of this cold

Of this cold and dark descending

Upon a heart

That is singing tunelessly

The blossoms are dumb

Without wonder

At the passing shadow

And the chilly gusts

Are borne as a momentary

Affliction that touches

Everything without

Specific malice

Toward everything

For the Year's End

Love is not here
And is nowhere found
That part of me which thought

As much of a fellowship with death
As life permits
Is all I now am

Through the door
Across the starry floor into
That which is neither

Darkness or light
And yet remains yearning
Not to be

In Consideration Of

I know that I
May be nothing beyond
The furthest star

Furiously burning
Bright and dim
But that star may be

Nothing at all
Ever becoming less
The light I see.

Lady Nova

It is when she is gone
Unimaginably wrong
Her subtle fecundity
Is the sudden catastrophe
Making radical days
That blind every eye to night
But not to see
And not to feel are
Death's blessing and best.

She is large upon the horizon
Of lands and waters
She is larger in her heaven
And oval golden white
Of light perpetual
The sea's significant end
The world hardly resists her turning
From lucid blue toward brown
Burned black.

Light Exuberance

The boy's mind
Was never more free
Than when he ran naked with the wind
There was the sound of his progress
Spanking the ground
And, that of his hard panting
There was the scent

Of the day becoming warm
And feel of it upon his skin
In it all the exhilarating
Sense of movement
There was above all
The light exuberance
Of his spirit running within him

Of it being of a mind
Apart from his mind
And yet wholly his own
And that spirit's
Swifter movement beyond
The body and into the air,
Invisibly clean

Love's Lyric

To press this warmth
Against your breast,

Is to know full well
How I am blest.

Mrs. Noe Meets Richard Wagner

He could not be

The world in the sense

That it is the place

Of the whole human event

Rather he became

Its master and giant

Straddling hemispheres

Northern and west

A superior order

That could impede

The progress of clouds

Diminish the stars

Or that could and did

Drink oceans dry

And at his end

How he rose

To eclipse the sun

With grandiloquent flourish

Turning those minds

That seek the wondrous

Toward himself and

This drama

Ideal.

The Moment Of Each Step

As I have waited, so shall I wait.
I know she will pass this way
Because I know she has passed every other way
Compelled by commission
To go where needed, where called
Cheerfully without hesitation
Often welcomed, more often unwelcomed
Nevertheless accomplishing her earnest best
Fully occupying the moment of each step.

As I have waited, I wait alone
Though I have not always waited alone

There were others dispersed
Throughout the tiers of known time
Whose span of tear wet days spilled
Each upon the other
Until desiccated through the expiration of ecstasy
They were not as I am
Sustained by anticipation
Sustained by the fragrance of a promise fulfilled
Tasking shadow of sweetness
Of things rare, unsearchable
Too exquisite to name

Imperishable things
Which are the content
Of my undreamt dreams

As I have waited, so I shall wait

According to an unconstructed confidence
Which substantiates my hope

With time, in time or without time
Until the time when such hope
Is no longer needed

The Necessity That Requires

You are wrong
To count me among
Their madly desperate men,
And to rank me again
With the low and myopic.
I am tired of trying.
To split hairs of time,
With no help beyond
My resources of mind.
I am tired of rolling
My eyes like dice,
Hoping to see past
The moment I'm in
And yet the whole of life
Seems worth the gamble
I must take,
For there is nothing less
Than living at stake.

Nor Light Reflecting Orb

Cold is their element

They strive toward

The perfections of zero

Has mother told you

The moon is not solid

Substance of earth

Is neither the servant

Of this world

Nor light reflecting orb

But is rather

The portal through which we pass

Upon the journey

That is death

And is death's peculiar light

Of the life beyond

O radiant round

That is nearer

The perfections of zero

Now the Fattest Poverty

The fattest man

Ever seen

Was once in orbit around

His beloved

And love it was

That made him immense

But now with his beloved lost

He drifts

Through the air of his despair

Like a mountain of grief

For loss

Has made him fatter.

October Greets the Virgins

It was a bit of both, of hope and fantasy
But hope nonetheless, that is now like

A promise realized. It is what you saw
In an August evening's aureate sky,

The day's decline, as night desires
That red and orange of twilight

Are the colors of autumn moving
In a vibrant costume of beautiful

But dead and dying leaves
Be glad in this October. Be glad

Of its pearl, of its gray and calm caresses
That soothe your cheek and dry

The tears you've shed in grief of summer
And of summer too large, implacable.

Regressive Biography

That book at midnight
Is yours to write

It is a project
You once abandoned

Take up the book
With words of yourself

Begin it again where
It seems to end

And write the pages
Blank and clean

Blanker for what
Is written therein

Compose it beneath
The starry north

But do so without
Moonlit romance.

Stop Midwinter to consider

I know

That I may be

Nothing beyond

The furthest star

Furiously burning

Bright and dim

But that star

May be nothing at all

Ever becoming

Less and less

The light

I see

That We Should Fast for A

Mister Z

Has made his pronouncements

In the moment that

These were spoken

His terrible heirs were born

He has not known them

But has heard

The noise they've become

Their striving crowd

Whatever else might be.

They are only the idea

Of what might follow Z

But nothing follows

Z was the strength

Of what came before

The last thing that caps

The column

His heirs have had children

They are furious

That the words of their fathers

Are less than this

Noise of air

What was it once

Where is it now

The passion that was B

Or that of C, G, and J

Or that of X

Who foretold with rage

The legacy

Of Z

Thank God for the Passage of Time

For better

Indeed,

That pleasure

Should end

And may yet

Be often

Relieved through memory

Than to have sorrow

Come, as it does

Perpetually,

And live this life

With cumulated

Grief.

That Would Be and Would Be Born

Pale is mountain's purple majesty
In a moment, it will fade from view
The snowy cap lengthens down.

Yes, it is beauty, different in kind,
But is cold beyond air.
In a moment, the pines will vanish,

Beneath the blight of snow,
Mountain once beheld itself
In the lake that laps its shore.

Now the waters darken
With that faded majesty,
And ice entombs the mountain.

But cold is not redemptive
The lake is red and blown
More turbulent for the wind

That wills to stir its waters
Wherein are children, that would be
And that would be born.

These Will Return Without Her

The great house maintains a dignity
Its mistress would approve
Though she is now past caring.
Her thoughts are of a natural order.
Not the small world of human hands
Her wide windows
Open to expanse of sky
To tracts of lawn and garden,
And to the trees
That were always her season
It was beauty for her
To think them most beautiful now
In their late autumn leaflessness
Memories of spring's
Copulative ways,
A summer boughs
Gold and green
Seemed less the things of memory
And more like some fiction
She imagined had once been real.
The gray clouds
And graying land
Seen through her bedroom windows
Are a monochrome

Of her sleep and waking
To windy music in the branches
Blown brown and black.
For her, the scene was peace.
She had no wish
To hear the red bird singing
Florid hymns,
But rather the elegance
Of trees standing
Intelligently against
Winter's decree.

Through Love Illumined

If it could be
The manifest power

Of its imagination
The very extreme and limit of time

And of desire's
Exquisite yearning

If it could conjure
And contain the scale

Of that fabulous machine
Which is the universe

How near and far it would be
In radiance to the sun

And stars and even beyond
Until they in turn

Become the dim and mere
Approximation

Of the terrible love

With which it loves

Through This First Maturity

Woman, it is that your golden crested soul,
Is the more certain treasure, than any such
    Quick or lucid sliver, that might

Comprise your mind. But you have believed
That dreams of life, give the living of life,
    All its hope and meaning.
    Daughter, you have grown with glory,
    But are yet my child, eternal.
    Thought may come with greater clarity
    But not in equal depth.

For you, thinking is to be and to begin.
    Before me, mortal thought is
Like ice forming in the first fans of cold,
    Before the zero chill settles

With illusory permanence. But it is the heart
Which changes conclusively: from riotous
Purple, through the days of dripping blue.

Despondency, toward this moments arrest, wherein
    You are free from thinking extremes
    Upon the mark of vivid ecstasy.

Woman's Words Are All of One

I

These nights and days of her sitting there
On the shore of her finite point are against
All dreams of my boundless depth.

I feel the intense scrutiny of my moods
In eyes that pierce my will and waver and are
Heavy upon my wind and sky.

It is the metaphysical weight of a
Physical desire for something within me
That gather in air above my seas.

II

She awakes at eventide as the sun sets
Amid its gaudy gold first
Enhanced then tempered by my hue.

Her figure recumbent upon that shore
Was the sense first of relief, then of grief
That her being was no part of mine.

It is that I was mother once but now there is air
I was mother and am still fecund
But it is not mine to be the mother eternal.

III

What I say is of a sentence hardly formed
The waters and waters the beach speaking
Words I collect in the wind that I might

Know more than her moonlit shadow
And starry elucidations
The sound of sound and sound euphoniums.

As she made these whispers and words of might:
"My pleasure begins with the old man's descent
But you, my seas, are no less a nurturer than he."

IV

"There shall be less of him now, or
Rather of his intensity as my heart's
Season is near: This splendid winter"

"Should be all of cool days and
Cooler nights. I embrace its every

Difficulty, no less the difficulty of myself."

"How odd that I remember the thinker
Who was also so much of wintry essence
Memory serves as comfort enough."

V

"Of him. The thought too much and though
The sun a brave man naked, traveling
Across the sky…Perhaps, brave."

"Indeed, to be so nude and yet like a god…
But no god is naked, nor in the sun
Cloaked in its coats of white-yellow gold."

"The concert is sure if I think him a god…
Such would ensample my mind's boundary,
To think so far and not beyond."

VI

"This desolate beach is hearty again
Subtly swept with star-lit secrets
So like me in design and repose."

"Something of the water is like the sound of night.
Of something shimmering that discloses itself.
As a kind of exquisite music, impossible to him."

"I should be such impossible music, if
My voice were the place of the sea,
The song in the waves, tempestuous or calm."

VII

"Moon…you are a glory degraded
As full of romance as the sun is of
The coarse and immediate."
"But your luminous chastity is the
Testimony of your innocence.
Of beauty bestowed and ever renewed."

"Your light is sufficient to make real,
The imagined. What is the divine about me…
But an excellence seeking itself without me."

VIII

"Taken in part, the sun and sky
Are whole in themselves, but one of lesser
Magnitude than my hearts reflection."

"Approved of these hushed majesties,
Of night-lit whispers upon the crest of waves…
It is to breathe of the infinite, quite ineffable."

"Moon…you aureate white becoming
Silver, in the danger of night's failing:
It becomes day too soon, again…"

IX

The dawn horizon is of such an eloquence
That it seems to extinguish the very stars
And fades the moon to the nearest crescent.

Or ghost of its midnight eminence
If the sun is that brave man returning.

What shall qualify night's grim luster

There are no birds or echo of birds
Resounding in this place at day-break
No grace of wings spread wide.

X

Light so like things imagined
Above my spray beneath the clouds
These tested the invariable real.

And were the possibility of music
Before her voice became my own
But birds would be a distraction here.

No matter the color of their cry
The woman's words are all of one
Like unto the praise that swells my waves.

Words of Herself

She wrote as she was in a book not her own
That had been abandoned by someone other.

Thus it was their work she might to complete
As she had none of her own so worthwhile (As she thought now…)

She wrote as she was what thus far was not written
Those things of herself that comprised herself.

It was however as difficult to write
As to write of sunset landscapes or

Of the sun's setting everywhere at once
To scribble the picture of mountain light fading

Required the heights of air an accurate view
Not that of eyes narrowed with tears or wit motes.

Of ocean evenings and the gleaming horizon
That there was water pond a great hazard

And in fear of the wind she became less than herself
The words of her being were thus not to be written.

UNTITLED

(A Black Bird's Domain)

I

Day has been
Overcast with
A threat of storm and wind
Nearby flocks
Of black birds
Have gathered.

II

A circle in perfection
A black bird circling overhead
Is perfection plus.

Fly down
Fly down dark thing
There is a woman waiting

For that shade
And gift of such knowledge
That you possess.

III

Fearful the sound
Of black wings beating

And is this sound
Of human hearts

That fail for fear
Beating furiously

IV

Are you certain
The angels were watching
As the two of you made love?

A black bird spied you
With curious indifference
It has concerns of its own.

V

In a park
Boy sits beneath
Midsummer's leafless boughs.

A black bird's lights
And wither above him
Its arrival is like
A dark idea
That is come to trouble
Boy's mind.

VI

Black birds
Do not migrate
They are here throughout
The year
Are they ever
The harbinger of a new season?

VII

Standing before
A tree that teems
With many black birds
A man and a woman
Are alone and

Are not one with the world

They are strangers and
Shall so remain
But they pause to wonder that
There are so many black birds.

VIII

Of the birds, yes
And now

A valley full of black birds
And when

Their wings
Are sudden into flight

The midday sky is the shadow
Of night.

IX

Outside her window
The black birds cry

Against the season's
Changing color.

But now bring

And black they appear again.

The snow and steadfast winter

Of her mast.

X

Unhappy farmer

Walk and weep

And curse loudly

Have wrought

Upon the wide acres

Of your corn.

XI

Surely now their children

Shall suffer

For many gone unto him

And because in that day

Men have become the cause

Of earth's grief.

Black birds shall have with their kin
A part in the earth's return
Of malice.

XII

It may be in October or July
It may be the morning after love
That opens upon a day of such brilliant light
That following upon a night of drenching rain
It may be and perhaps so
But there is also that December day
Of black birds coming

Untitled

(Bagatelle)

The day was dark
Autumnal gray
Crows were gathered
In the trees
And raucously called
One to another
As they lit from
Branch to branch

Some people think
Them a nuisance
Others might think
Them a pest
The farmer believes
They're a plague

The day was dark
And was like
Evening stretched
From dawn to dusk
And seemed the darker
For this presence
Of crows.

Untitled
(Bliss)

Upon the night
He would sleep
In the calm sense
Of life's deepest satisfaction

But he would not dream
Of waking pleasures
Neither would there be
Nightmares of that

Impending grief
Which is so much
This world's wasted beauty
And content of vulgar blessing

Only the most familiar darkness
Would be before his eyes and
A last thoughtful wondering
What is life tomorrow?

Untitled

(Ebony Queen)

How rare
That ebony queen, called
Never such love
By her people
How she was
The soul of compassion,
And compassionate

To a fault
The way she wove
Her hands through the air
With nails painted
Yellow-orange
As if her fingers
Had been dipped in sunlight

Her gowns and jewelry
Were hardly worthy
Of her
But such were the token
Of her people
And part of what their love
Could bestow

Untitled

(Fuel for Time)

He waits
But wants for nothing more,
And is grown old

Beyond the number of his years.
He is that shell
And shadow of a man

Who has lost his life
Through life's necessity
What others have had

He has had
The light of what might have been
And shade of what

Might yet be…
But all that he would possess
Is less and less than

Nothing but…
As he is, his yet
Fuel for time and time's burning

Untitled
(Give What We Cannot)

It is a sad and terrible life
We live wherein we cannot give
What we want and cannot give
What is required.

We have been there
And have had there.

We there have
Had their sorrows
In love.

Not to give
As we would want
To what

What we cannot have
And to be asked to give
What we cannot.

And we cannot
Give what we don't
Possess.

Untitled

(Her Reply of No)

He asked her why
She replied simply no

He became for insistent
Again she said no

He began to shout
She quietly said no

He asked her once more
But she'd become silent

She'd spoken her peace
In her mind she thought

That his questions might
Turn her pages

But her no
Closed the book.

Untitled

(It May Be October)

It may be October

It may be July

It may be a spring morning that opens

To the brilliant light

That follows a night of drenching rain

It may be and perhaps so

But there is also that December day

Of black birds coming.

Untitled

(The Man In His Room)

There is

The man in his room

That is

A worm in its cocoon

Thinking and the myriad

Things of himself,

Are the slime in which he writhes

Night is a cause of fear

That prevents

That depth of sleep

Wherein he might dream

The possible metamorphosis

With night comes

A ravenous bird

It picks and pecks

The remains of day

And fills its craw

With sweet fruit

But better now to have the bitter worm

The more satisfying

For having been formed

                                                  January 1994

Untitled

(Perhaps)

Perhaps,
An old poet's
Last enterprise
Might be
An attempt
To recapture
That zest

Which perceived
All the life
Of this earth as
The ground
Potential poem
Then again
That last effort

Might be
Little different
From the first,
To ever reconcile
The self
To the world through
The life of words.

Untitled

(Sacrifice)

But…I shall give my body up
To be burned…And this shall be
Done for love. For love is

Our hope and grief, and is
The golden sorrow that has grown
So furious and bright between us…

When was oblivion so sweetly proffered,
That in becoming less ourselves,
We are more, the one.

Part III
Revelations

A Last Word For Lazarus

St. John X1

HE ESTABLISHED NIGHT THAT WE MIGHT KNOW HIS LIGHT

This mist, the vapor of my life,
Dissipates in the warm lengthening of light
Of infinite spring, where our first garden
Blooms continuously with deepening iridescence.

Lord, my desire is satisfied.

From the first word, I was shown Your salvation.
And the contentment I have known, has strength
To deliver me from the moment of this perishing dream,
Into what is substantial, into what is actual…

Into the brightness of illimitable joy unspeakable.

Such things, of the withering world,
Running streams nourished of the ice-caped mountain,
The cry of the newborn, the slaughter of the innocent,
The softening evening sun glistening through
Sweet blown hair, children's laughter,
Woven together, were brilliant music
Deeply felt.

But now these echo,
Hushed thunder out of distant lightning.

The lengthening light cast shadows I have known before,
And illuminates memory of the astonishment
At having been carried away by the curse—
Which no covenant has yet voided—
Surpassed only by the greater bewildered wonder
At being restored to this dimension,
Upon the authority of three small words.

My kinsmen have rolled away the stone,
Have rolled away the stone, a third time
And the waiting sepulcher has been prepared
According to custom, according to ritual.

Let these lips, once pursed for kiss,
Now become cold and numb, pursed in prayer,
Smile in the extreme moment
Of my evanescent passion.
And when that intensity has passed,
Let the truth I have live and spoken remain,
Unsullied by exaggerations of personality.
A testimony, an inheritance.

Lord, my eyes close to what is present

And search the past which is my future.

Exchanging the moment affliction

Of this perishing dream, for the surpassing peace

Found beyond the undreamt dream.

A Man Was Caught Up And Saw

II Corinthians XII:1-4

…a man was caught up and saw….

Who was before
And was born
Out of an infinite moment
When compassion
Was spoken to action

Who stood within
And after the terror
Who walked with time
To arrest the error

Who moves within a vortex bright
Behind clouds of cascading light
Who is seated upon an aureate throne
Shining more vibrantly
Than flaring stars have shone
Against the veil of infirm night

….there was thunder and not thunder….

Behind the near

And distant firmament
Fixed as a shroud
Before a brightening scene
An expanse of time suspended
By an assemblage of angels
And of the ancients
Who roar and roll the elements
As a master musician
Performs with virtuosity
Resplendent figures
Their form translucent
Each being suffused of light
Modulating only
In degrees of brightness
As they pass through ecstasy
Into ecstasy
Still and moving

Across the arced horizon
Raining down stars
With hands that spread the nebula
Reflecting the eternal glory
Within a single moment
As they burnish morning
To lucid sterling
To set it as a crown

Upon all the small days
Which passed before

…and there was thunder not thunder…

…heard with ears given to hear
        not ears of flesh,
                but of a substance
                more substantial…
…and there was thunder not thunder of ten thousand
                times ten thousand and a thousand tongues

        in exaltation…

He is the music
Morning sang down

Heard in the chirping
Of drab little birds
Seen in the sway
Of the ripening stalk
Bowed under the weight
Of its fruit

His melody warmed
The frozen air

As a distant violin
Sweetens the still of the night
And shook the zero tyrants
From their webs of ice

He is the music
Sung down again

The only music
That moves without time
Accompanying the dancers
Dancing upon the waves of glass
Having had no knowledge
Of the pattern of steps
Until they yielded
To His pulse

And there
The wind was roused and swirled down
To gather the cries and whispers of stone
And rock as they made response
To the music that walked among them

And the wind
Slid about as it willed
Listening for the beat of expectant hearts

And curled about them
To give comfort

And folded
The disparate voices in counterpoint
Against ebullient heaven
Drawing all
Into a fine still point

After the thunder
The cloud of witness fell prostrate and dumb
At the Word whispered
Out of the wind filled silence.

Before the Final Gold

After all
This man of fortune
Shall be among
The very fortunate

In that he desired
A bliss imperishable
Which was from inception
Deeply fulfilled.

He held to desiring it
Pertinaciously
And walked with its clarity
Ever before him.

After all
This man of fortune
Shall be among
The very fortunate

In that he desired a bliss imperishable
Which was from conception
Completely fulfilled

He held to desiring it
Pertinaciously
And walked with its radiance
Ever before him.

The Days Are Passing Strange

What does it portend?
That a mid-winter's day
Should occur at the bright of summer
And be more strange for the snow
That falls within it, more golden than
The color of the setting sun?

Is it that there is not
Enough sense of wonder, that this wintry
Glistening lingers longer, out of its season
Despite the warmth and length of days?
The little doctor studies.
Comparing text with that.

And yet in rooms that glow with
Brighter candle-light, he hardly knows
What he has read. Snow in August…
A fool, there is, the last in the line of oracles.
He sees and sings the revelation
Of the unknown God.

Divine Characters

He concludes

With the following:

"Yet, none of you

Should fault or begrudge

Even this dreamer

His wildest dreams…

For despite having been

Vexations tool

He nonetheless holds you

In great esteem

He is thus before you

Toward the goal and diadem

Worthy of life…

You should do well

To take example

And be blest to walk the gold of

His favor…to have

His dream of life

Break upon your days

That together you might live

Within that light…

Your taunts to torment

Are indeed, small matter,

Even those that have dealt death…

As in that eternal mind

You are clothed

Not with the shame

Of late misdeeds

But rather with the robe of

His grave regard,

Tempered and glistening with threads of mirth

And are clean

For such love…

Elegy

It was…

     The exquisite charm of her company,
Which worked a pleasant power
Dispelling those dark unprofitable meditations
So easily aroused, that clamorously crowd
Each lonely moment, every solitary hour.

     The exquisite charm of her conversation,
The constant gracious affirmation
Of what I had hoped to find in the feminine,
Luxuriously quieting my unspoken
Puerile romantic notions.

     The exquisite charm of her countenance
Its beauty fresh, reminiscent of first flowers
Never brighter than when she enjoyed
The full expression of my ardor
Attentive to the every whisper of my heart.

     Theses and the thousand particulars of her grace
The sweet testimony that she was
The virtuous wife of Proverbs
The embodiment of that biblical ideal.
     An exquisitely charming creature.

Of An Elegy
(A Moment After)

Now, you see the angel descends,
And demons foolishly aspire
As they move, they coruscate, each

Ascending to their depth of being
One burns with malice, the other with wrath
But you are the scene's principal character.

See, your lifeless form is fallen.
With fear, with bewildered wonder
Behind it like, the doomed daughter

Who turned to watch her great cities burning
But drink the peace and revelation
That follow upon your angry death.

The truth therein shall displace myth,
And is more for you in a moment than
Diana's daughters might ever dream.

The angel, your angel, descends.
See how bright you've become.
The demon aspires but has nothing in you.

See, the flesh succumbs to blight, deprived
As it in of spirit…But now ascend
And be above angels and demons.

Genesis 11:4

Who knows this passing glory of…

Thinking of a people
Building a tower
Toward their dream
Of paradise
Is thinking of people
Building towers
That comprise their paradise

A world of passion without compassion

Light Crescendo

I remember,

You stood in a lighted crevice
Between two shadows,
Barely discernible.

(Were such shadows the remnant
Of things I prized, dimmed and
Surpassed by your luster?)

Were you always there,
Obscured by the noise of hollow desire?

And, with a sudden crescendo,
Your nourishing touch
Drew me away from remote places to self
To know that which stretched before
And reaches after…

Is death.

Made Greater

And you withdrew

A figure folded into the shimmering rhythm

Of broken angels

But you have been made greater than angels

You have been made to know greater glory

Than the fever that spreads their wings

To crowd the wounded air

With a fortissimo of coruscating stars

After the rending caress

And the deep press

Of lips, when warn breath

Becomes breathless, return in knowledge

Of the communion which flames old blood

And cold spirit to chastity and silence

Until the deft light glistens

Upon the dove feather

To satisfy the end of searching eyes

To the purpose of good

And not evil.

November Light

He is the warmth
Of autumn sunshine
That arrests the cold

That would stiffen our bones
But he is beyond
Extremes of mind, and yet lives

Well within the heart's memory where
We knew him before
The burden of being

Think of This, Then That

After all, this man of fortune
Is among the most fortunate

That he desired a bliss, imperishable
Was from inception, deeply fulfilled

He held to desiring it, pertinaciously
And walked with its clarity, ever before him.

Thirty-three Preludes

For My Father

I

The preludes are of music past
What remains is to perfect the present
To know the why of what is not
Is the wealth of tears.

II

Hear the lesser instruct the greater
The chameleon is pleased to teach
Novice birds the use of their iridescent plumage
Fly only into brightest daylight
Night is not among your colors.

III

Less bread, more wine
The year's grapes are abundant
With sweeter juice than last
However, they suffice the lack of wheat.

IV

Silvered with frost and frosted hair
That shone as if diamond-flecked
She was the believer's beautiful dream
And comprised a past
Of the joy in believing.

V

The verdure of this place is not as it was
Set ignorant boys about the task
Of extracting green from emerald light.

VI

Fat mother, remember
The price of your baby's fat perfections.

VII

Naked ignoble Salome
Stand and plead your innocence.

VIII

The lamb bit the lion's tail
And lion did not turn to bite it back
Now pragmatic pessimists
Are able to think
The possible yes.

IX

You do not dine alone
But take your meals with your monster
You eat your fill but are never satisfied
But the beast is satisfied
To feast upon you.

X

She is sentimentalist
Pressing petals of a single rose
Between pages of her memory's book
She is also realist
Pressing there besides a thorny stem.

XI

What glistened seemed more
The stream's swift life
Than any reflected light.

XII

Her Music director
A deft virtuosity might tame cacophony
With an unassuming tune
But this fiddler brakes his fiddlesticks
Striving against the din.

XIII

Who was the woman walking
With Diana and with Eve
Arrayed in purple praise
Washed red with tears
Making the motions of song.

XIV

Look

It's Georges Ratatoville

But no

Isn't he dead?

The thing that's killed him

Seems exactly like him

Or was he always more dead

Than alive?

XV

If virgins walk the beach in winter

They walk there pursuing

More exquisite pleasure

Observed only by the one

To whom this chastity is pledged.

XVI

The sun is patron gold and connoisseur

To earth's blue and perfect potential.

XVII

The actual masterpiece

Is painted with

Imagination's in tensest reds

That originate in the very blood.

XVIII

Besides this melon there is

More succulent fruit

Ripe to plunk from life

Sweeter apples too than those she chose

Their meat is pulpy and tart.

XIX

What is and not is all the poem

Of God.

XX

A scent of heat

Will possess a season

It should then be dampened

Before it becomes the cause of need.

XXI

It is deeper music
That music imitator
The wind upon the water
Sighs Kyrie Eleison
Men will hardly hear.

XXII

Day knows night's
depth of darkness
Night knows the end of light
But after holy holocaust
One shall remain
And neither shall know the other.

XXIII

Herodias distract yourself from nagging care
Cook up that rich confection
Of bread cream and black bananas.

XXIV

To walk there and pray aloud
Amid the crash and crescendo
Of wind and wave is
The precise aspect of heaven's praise.

XXV

Other ignorant boys busy themselves
With the task of extracting the pale from sapphire skies
Let imagination make
The mind superfluous.

XXVI

Willing anaphrodisia
The fire goes out of virgins
Long before they are old with age
Hands that come to caress
Are hands of the grotesque

XXVII

Kitten
Lay the dead mouse

At your mother's feet
While she purrs her accolades
The mouse-fellows give grief no pause
But continue their dance
In the kitchen.

XXVIII

The scent of flowers and drift of petals
Complete and compliment
The depth and brightness of air.

XXIX

The believer cannot believe
That virgins long for snow in June
Or that they fondly remember December
But cold is their fortune
And the end of desire.

XXX

Bid the old women
Put down their cats
And take up the shining trombones

Have them play an aequale
Not as solemn finale but as prelude
To more splendid magnitude.

XXXI

Consider the mountainous hazard
Of life and living to be
In relationship to faith
As the giant was to Jack.

XXXII

The hierarchies of angels
The resounding fortissimo
Of their call into being
But thinking these things
Is greater than angels.

XXXIII

The believer thinks
Of Sunday mornings

Of the thunderations of organ and choir

And thinks again and

Thinks again

Of the sparrow's sterling abode.

Thus Shall the Angels Be Judged

I am bright
With glory and
Bright with the favor set
To shine before
Upon and after you.

Yes, I fly forward
To perfect your future
And return to preserve this present
All in the power of
His abiding Host.

I am this answer
To your questions regarding
What is possible?
And what is love?
Infinitely personal.

Toward Heavenly Credence

I

Author and master builder is
Same spirit of the house
Upon which love is lavished and
Nearest expression of being.
In his garden, spiders spin

To make jewelry of the morning dew
Together with silk and sun.
There the lamb rest with the lion.
The great beast is made more majestic
For its strength of repose.

The author and finisher is
Beauty, he is one with his name.
That which is seen and unseen,
Even things grotesque are,
Beauty's profound measure.

II

Heaven is bliss in that it ignores
Earthly music that would supplant.
For music is the arch that reaches
Toward this world and worlds beyond,
And thing of earth most heaven like.

Think what music there is to accompany
The dancers dancing on the sea of glass…
Think what music shall inform
The magnificent day of marriage feast…
And every angel shall take up a trumpet

To make a stellar hymn as
Holy groom presents his bride
To the sovereign host…
Choir and organ, through stained glass,
Must suffice 'til heaven is heard.

III

Remember the Adam that
Was the father of sorrow.
He died to die again through
Catastrophe wrought of desire.

The Adam was sapphirine man

And very blue of lost worlds' turning.
Despondent man among men
And weight of despair that comes,
Unable to shed tears.
Man for whom the promise came,

Knows that love is no better made
For mercy moves through the garden,
That is yet his to keep.
That mercy is no matter of moments, but
The needful condition of being.

IV

The house invisible
Built upon the invisible rock.
The house may be found
By as many that are led,
Become as children again.

The house invisible
Become indivisible
Upon the rock of the mind,
In accord with hearts

Become child-like again.

Pray the master, lessen these walls,
To accommodate the curios crowd
Drawn by the mirth
And peculiar ideal,
Of them that gather therein.

V

Children are a joy of the place,
With nursery rhyme nonsense
And laughing games.
Given into angelic care,
Babies and older yearn

Toward their first maturity.
But count among the despised,
Among the abused, those misused,
Prematurely cut from the womb,
A part of tragedy gone full term.

But faith is large with children.
Their eyes like crystals, into which one might peer,
Retain no pain nor malice suffered.
Only an absolute knowledge of good,

And see the present, perfected.

VI

Because history is repetition.
The world should weary
Of words that whirl it about.
What has been spoken
To form lasting foundation?

Poets cannot count as such,
Their words are those of the muse.
Prophets cannot count as such,
With care they spoke not their own.
Paradise is an inspired word.

Spoken once and still bearing
The first force of personality.
The word secures eternity or
Withheld it is cause enough
For tears to dissolve the world.

VII

You were Eve and you are Eve.
Restored to heavenly estate,
And to the eternal paradise
Which is actual and is also
The minds' common notion.

As paradise is given you,
You are the gift of paradise.
The air, green with a late spring's progress,
Is in union with the garden and
Your heart's emerald essence.

You are nakedness unadorned,
Translucent made transparent,
For the jewel within that shines without,
That is next in light to love
And to love's perfection.

VIII

Autumn come as prescribed,
In most gaudy costume.
Come in windy chants, though
Not to harbinger death.

Come as festive, in celebration of
All that heaven's accomplished.
Come in such colors that
Rival memories of spring.
Swell a crescendo
Into fortissimo and

Litter the leaves like confetti…
Bid winter come, a brilliant white
But without white's extremes, to be
Heaven's adagio phrase,
Season of cool quiescence.

IX

You are Eve, first bride and mother,
Now mother again of the bride
Gathered from earth's every corner.
The bride that is indeed
Last remnant of the natural world.

The natural world grown so unnatural
That the bride would be
With violence expelled if not
Caught away at the blast of a trumpet…
Like the twinkling of an eye
A flash illuminates

The whole world at once but
The shimmer is of dark revelation:
The light of the present world
 Is also caught away…

X

It is the festival of the last things.
History's culmination and
Celebration for the end of time…
Or as the finite mind designs,
Beginning of the eternal age.

With that of heaven's host,
Eve has bestowed her blessing
Upon the groom and his bride.
Nothing higher can be conferred except,
That which the groom shall give…

And he has given himself to history,
To secure the place of his bride…
Stars, given pause and sing a welcome.
Make a resplendent music with you light as
Groom turns to set the bride above you…

A Word To Mrs. Noe

People are poison…
When one day is
The light of a thousand
Summer afternoons.
This dust of earth
Shall be the black
Of your starless nights.
God is antidote…

People are poison…
When one day is the light of a thousand
Summer afternoons
This dust of earth
Shall be the black
Of your blinded days.
God is antidote…

Untitled

(Both Judge and Advocate)

Then,
My Lord Nether, stood
To address the court.
That the assembly
Might be put in remembrance
Of that which was spoken.
I am now

The first counsel
To the king's mind.
My eyes are the gift
Of dark clairvoyance
And narrow light
Into the heart of the kingdom
Thus, all are naked before me

But without shame.
I discern the virtue of each and allow
Those conflicts of soul which are a part
Of your perfecting and service.
It is that this knowledge
Of my person and office
Should work to dispel mystery.

Untitled

(Eve)

Eve, history has become
Naught but repetition
And the world wearies of the words
That whirl it about
Mother of generations

What does heaven speak
The words of the prophets
Are nearly lost to us
And those of the poets
Are nearly too hard for us

So near to inspiration
Heaven must know and confide
That which secures eternity
Or is cause enough for tears
To dissolve the world.

Untitled

(Eve II)

Eve, you know the fragrance
Of a burning rose and
The velvet caress of its petals
Upon your cheek as well as you know
The sudden prick of thorns

And the bitter consequence of desire
Of that for man and then for God
And terrible ecstasy of desirous fulfillment
You were Eve and you are Eve
Woman and mother eternal

Of the first Adam after God
And generations born after God
In heaven you now know
The different ecstasy of compassion
That is the network of empathetic souls.

Untitled

(The Lovers Lost)

It is to have been
Wrong so long
That profound error seems

The truest course
Therefore pray the father
That his judgement be

Exercise of unrighteousness
The lovers are beyond each other's reach
And only have their object

Their bliss and mystical dream
Of fulfillment
Therefore pray the father and

Make such supplication that
Things contrary to the lovers be
So known, the enemy alien

James Edward Jordan

James Edward Jordan was born April 5, 1960 in Milwaukee, Wisconsin to Lee Andrew Jordan, Jr. and Ethel Marie Sims. James attended the Milwaukee Public School system and later graduated from the University of Wisconsin-Stout.

Following his brother to New York City, James settled in Brooklyn, New York. James worked as an administrator in Finance. He also participated in producing various theater, film and television productions in New York and New Jersey. James currently resides in Central New Jersey with his wife, Carmen, of over 25 years.

www.ingramcontent.com/pod-product-compliance
Lightning Source LLC
Chambersburg PA
CBHW070814100426
42742CB00012B/2354